F

MW00584145

"A spell-binding touchstone of poetry, Christina Sng's done it again! This book of poems is evocative, haunting, surprising and heart-breakingly poignant. Her use of language is exquisite. Every word counts in the brevity of her poetry. Her minimal poems reflect the strength of thoughts and emotions that comprise the worlds she creates. *The Gravity of Existence* is a must read!"

—t.santitoro, editor, Scifaikuest

"Christina Sng's *The Gravity of Existence* is a rapture of profound, visceral emotions, gutted on the page in all their glory. Her terrors cut deep, some playing with the undead, while others run colder like shafts of darkness that penetrate the reader's heart. Her poems, as ever, are sublime."

—Eva Roslin, writer and reviewer

"Christina Sng is the Emily Dickinson of tiny genre verse. Her new collection is simply delightful. For example: "vampiric fog/ the forgotten tales/ of anemia," or "thrown away in recycling/ glass slippers stained with blood/ from the stepsisters'/severed toes." Some thought-provoking, philosophical, others have you smiling without realizing. Whether you're in flight above the earth, or simply in a mood to be fantastically regaled, there's many a poem you'll enjoy! A fitting addition to your bookcase from an award-winning poet."

—Marge Simon, multiple Bram Stoker winner, author of *Victims*

THE GRAVITY OF EXISTENCE

POEMS

by Christina Sng

THE GRAVITY OF EXISTENCE

Edited by Holly Lyn Walrath.

Cover art by Anna Surgan.

Published by Interstellar Flight Press
Houston, Texas.

www.interstellarflightpress.com

ISBN (eBook): 978-1-953736-16-1
ISBN (Paperback): 978-1-953736-17-8

For my children

May the gravity of existence
Never weigh heavy on you
But feel light and free
As the stardust we are

To Dad, who taught me that brevity is everything.

TABLE OF CONTENTS

Prelude 1

The Gravity of Loss 3

Sand Under a Microscope 4

Escape 5

Real Monsters 7

Sparrow 9

Monstress 10

The Monsters at Home 11

Monsters 12

Blood 13

The Joy of Traveling 15

Body Parts 16

A Better World 17

Childhood Tales 19

Little Red in Haiku 21

Snow White 22

Sleeping Beauty 22

Rapunzel 22

Cinderella 23

Goldilocks and the Three Bears 24

Puss in Boots 24

Hansel and Gretel 24

The Wizard of Oz 25

Dorothy 25

Alice in Wonderland 25

The Werewolf 26

Basilisks 26

The Siren 27

Medusa 27

The Snow Queen 27

Ghost Stories 29

Marriage 31

Fears 32

Ghosts 33

Magic 34

The Enlightenment of Science 35

Electroconvulsive Therapy Session One 37

Dead Alive 38

Cages 39

A New Earth 40

In Sickness, In Death 41

Ebola Virus 43

Mass Murders 44

First Day of Summer 45

The Graveyard 46

The Immortality of Stars 47

The Gift 48

The End 49

The Darkness 50

Rare Peaceful Day 51

Nuclear 52

Asteroid 53

All Are Welcome 54

How We Die 55

Life on Kepler-452b 56

All That We Love 57

The Many Ways We Die in Space 58

Alien Worlds 59

Cats in Space 60

Life in Space 61

Aliens 62

Mysteries of Space 63

Beyond 64

Found Footage 65

Requiem 67

Requiem 69

Acknowledgments 71

Awards 75

About the Author 77

About the Cover Artist 79

Interstellar Flight Press 80

PRELUDE

THE GRAVITY OF LOSS

It was sheer luck that you took flight 250 and I, flight 851. How grateful I am that we made up before we parted, as I now sob uncontrollably, watching your plane engines sputter and fail, free-falling.

the age-old battle
between force and gravity
the gravity of loss

SAND UNDER A MICROSCOPE

The loveliest of all collections
Lies under a microscope.
In a handful of sand,
A treasure trove:

Tiny amoebic shells
Frozen in time;
Petrified wood
Frightened of life;

Rare azure quartz
Lost in the ocean;
A crystal wishbone,
Perfect and unbroken;

The treasure of this collection.

ESCAPE

"Why do you read
The moment you get home?"
I ask my child, her nose in a book.

"To escape the horrors
Of the world," she says.
I nod and we exchange a look.

REAL MONSTERS

SPARROW

I turn into a sparrow
When the sky turns gray.

I cover the ground
With a blanket of red.

Vengeance is sweet
When slowly pecked.

I savor the taste.
It's been a long wait.

MONSTRESS

turning my skin
inside out
laundry day

dust carpet
my monster imprint
under the bed

keepsakes I treasure
pinned on the wall
your flayed skin

snowy plains
so hard to hide
a blood trail

unrelentlessly
the blood rain falls
routine decapitation

THE MONSTERS AT HOME

childhood monster
standing before me
ordering coffee

black moon
another mysterious
bruise

a hundred
soul-draining years
of living
with a wraith
the price of dark magic

MONSTERS

hoping
the steel windows
will keep them out
this time
iteration 25365

bones fusing back again
head wound healing
brain regenerating
suicide #245628—failure
the curse of immortality

gritting my teeth
so they can't remove another
underground torture chamber

all my nightmares
saved in the dream catcher
I hang over your bed

wrong turn
a cemetery
of open graves

BLOOD

the strange sensation
of no longer needing to breathe
first day as a vampire

sunset
she eagerly awaits
her first feed

the second
taste of blood
always better

vampiric fog
the forgotten tales
of anemia

finally having fun
at the vampire mixer
the maddening dawn

all this rain
stuck in my coffin
all night again

mesmerized
by sunlight
child vampire

THE JOY OF TRAVELING

Go see the world, they said.
It'll be fun, they said.

Stranded on a ship
With nothing left to eat
And no one to navigate.

Lost seasick vampire.

Body Parts

the wine
much sweeter
this year
all those corpses
in the vat

                    root cellar
                    the bodies age
                    nicely

first date
finding a head
in her freezer

                    tree on a hill
                    the corpse
                    feeds it well

sprinkled beneath
my favorite tree
your lovely bones

A BETTER WORLD

I cast a magic spell
To manifest my grief,
Creating a new world
Full of rage-filled ghouls
Bent on protecting girls.

CHILDHOOD TALES

LITTLE RED IN HAIKU
A joined poem

flash of red
through the woods
alarums

old goat
tougher than expected
long lunch

sweetness
of maraschino cherries
baby smells

roleplaying
another species
something new

calmness
tenderizes the meat
grandma not grandma

clear anomalies
the sharpness of teeth
and claws

the speed
of younglings
chest arrow

her sobs
as he fades to black
grandma bones uncovered

SNOW WHITE

red apples
on a wooden sill
stepdaughter arriving

SLEEPING BEAUTY

bloody spindle
putting another princess
under again

RAPUNZEL

rappelling
for the first time
rapunzel

CINDERELLA

midnight
one slipper
missing again

thrown away in recycling
glass slippers
stained with blood
from the stepsisters'
severed toes

even as queen
still a sneaker kind of girl
cinderella

GOLDILOCKS AND THE THREE BEARS

after their walk
the bears discover something
tastier than porridge

PUSS IN BOOTS

a cat walking upright
down the street wearing boots
now I've seen everything

HANSEL AND GRETEL

racing out
of the woods
a boy and a girl
swear off candy
for life

The Wizard of Oz

tornado warning
putting on my red shoes
just in case

Dorothy

yellow bricks
on this road
she takes
the ruby express
instead

Alice in Wonderland

autumn moon
a cat fades in
a cat fades out

THE WEREWOLF

pet wolf
refusing to sit
full moon

BASILISKS

garage sale
the stone basilisks stare
disapprovingly

THE SIREN

tidal waves
broken heart
of the siren

MEDUSA

found in Sarpedon
a lost child
with snakes for hair
the world soon
turns to stone

THE SNOW QUEEN

lofty silver statuettes
on winter's ice
exquisite corpses

GHOST STORIES

Marriage

Every day,
I brush against you
But you never notice.
Things haven't changed
That much since I died.

FEARS

soft whispers
outside my home
shallow graves

standing still
at dusk
her shadow shifts

sheets flapping
my childhood fears
reignite

the dogs won't stop
barking at nothing
ghost month

GHOSTS

old photo
all those years
we thought
the ghost
was just a smudge

midnight
philosophical conversations
with my dead grandmother

bringing
my kitty back
from the grave
I promised her
I'd never leave her

longing
to be extinguished
every single day
thousand-year-old ghost
still trapped at home

MAGIC

witching hour
my daughter reads
the spellbook aloud

solar eclipse
the dead rise
from the shadows

whispered words
from genetic memory
my dead cat alive again
the forgotten art
of necromancy

spellbook spent
finally accepting
that dead is dead

animate dead things
zombie apocalypse
sorry world

THE ENLIGHTENMENT OF SCIENCE

ELECTROCONVULSIVE THERAPY SESSION ONE

Remember it now
In all its terrible glory.

Send current through brain.
Awful memory erased.

Ready?
Remember the next.

DEAD ALIVE

head still reeling
at how they did it
baby boy in my arms

                              dead butterfly
                              flaps its wings
                              revival potion works

CAGES

keeping you
in a Faraday Cage
favorite android

                    3D printing a better world

alone on the space station
the chill in my blood
when I hear footsteps

A NEW EARTH

News alert: the inception of spontaneous wormholes on Earth
turns science experiments awry.

yet again
Schrödinger's cat vanishes
from the glass box
only to reappear
beside its food bowl

IN SICKNESS, IN DEATH

EBOLA VIRUS

It moves on.
Why does its host
Always expire?

It wonders,
Is it me
Or is it them?

MASS MURDERS

kill order approved
the ground flora
releases neurotoxins

                    flu pandemic
                    the wind blows
                    an empty swing

First Day of Summer

Low tide
Beneath the blinding sunlight.

In a watery alcove by the shore,
She finds a chest of treasure
And bones of the man she lost.

THE GRAVEYARD

Walking through
The graveyard,
I wept rivers of tears
For the brave souls lost
Battling the humans.

THE IMMORTALITY OF STARS

made of star stuff
every death
still hurts

> star clusters
> my children and I
> huddle together

clinically dead
the brain dreams
in remnants

> sky full of stars
> wishing
> I could live
> long enough
> to visit them all

THE GIFT

My body no longer
Listens to my brain,
The tether they had
Slowly unraveling.

Death's cold hand
Reaches out for me
And to my surprise,
I take it.

THE END

THE DARKNESS

I let go of the darkness
That dwelt in my heart

And it blanketed the sky
In a permanent night.

That was how the world died.

RARE PEACEFUL DAY

Rare peaceful day
He removes his headphones

        Outside—
           half of Earth
               has been blasted away.

NUCLEAR

Fukushima
snow rabbit
patient zero

> Chernobyl
> three-headed wolves
> survey their territory

after
the radiation leak
as if my arachnophobia
could not get worse
sixteen-foot spiders

> bus-sized geckos
> fatted from feasting
> bask by the sandy coastline
> among trampled hammerhead bones
> we walk back to the radiation plant

in a flash
a hand of ash in mine
apocalypse

ASTEROID

seconds before
the asteroid hits
he finally tells me
he loves me
eye roll

mega-tsunami
after the disaster
a fresh start

meteor shower
how we were
infected

ALL ARE WELCOME

Everyone was mostly polite
Through their clicking sounds
And pincer-like arms

But we drew a line when
The alien couple decided
To have our brains for lunch.

Their banishment began
An interplanetary conflict
That turned Mars red

And ended the First Age of Man.

How We Die

electricity
in the sky
alien warships

                              flickering flame
                              from a matchstick
                              our dying sun

the graying skies
the rising tide
from the mountains
we watch the world die
minute by minute

                              sun death
                              the end of things
                              a new beginning

LIFE ON KEPLER-452B

I could not help
Bringing home a flower
From Kepler-452b.

No one ever imagined
Earth's extinction
Would be by pollen.

ALL THAT WE LOVE

I wake up
From hibernation
On a new planet

Mourning my lovey
Who didn't survive
The thousand years.

THE MANY WAYS WE DIE IN SPACE

too quickly
he leaped joyfully
into the alien sea
we needed no readings
to realize it was acid

                                            first night on our new planet
                                            the death mist takes us
                                            fifth element of Kepler b

within sight
before our engines died
Proxima Centauri

ALIEN WORLDS

ruby sky
first day
as a Martian

                              the song I can't
                              get out of my head
                              stasis chamber

just wanting
to see blue skies again
Arcturus orbit

                              seeing red
                              all day
                              Antares orbit

CATS IN SPACE

a world
of possibilities
my cat in a box

                still can't decide
                whether to go in or out
                our cat hovers
                by the entrance
                of our escape pod

watching the last
space shuttle leave
our feet gently
kneading the blue grass
me and my cat

LIFE IN SPACE

after hypnotherapy
my abduction
comes back to me
the moon of Kepler-16b
still bright in my eyes

running reels of my children
on loop in my helmet cam
final hour of air
on the ruptured
Jupiter space station

silent orbit of stars
the harmonious spheres
of my baby mobile

...time loop
repeating
the same mistakes
over and over
…time loop

wishing
I had died with them
last survivor
of Space Ark One
on Kepler 22-b

ALIENS

alien sapling
quietly growing
in another pot

                            still biting me
                            the moth-sized mosquitoes
                            on Mars

age-old battle
in the skies of Jupiter
cloud leviathans

                            during the long years
                            far from the sun
                            I sleep
                            dormant from the cold
                            lifeform on Planet X

immortality
just one drop of blood
from the alien

MYSTERIES OF SPACE

the many ways
I should be dead
parallel universes

          in my hands
          millions of micro universes
          seaside sand

emerging
seemingly unharmed
from a wormhole
part of me wonders
am I still me

        multiverse theory this feeling of déjà vu

BEYOND

starlight in my eyes
during my final breaths
hull breach

> slow boat to the stars
> the humans
> we began with
> not the same humans
> who arrive

the feeling
like time is standing still
supermassive black hole

> our ships
> sail past the horizon
> and into deep space
> type III
> kardashev civilization

FOUND FOOTAGE

There goes our last wrench

Tumbling away into space,
And now our engineer with it.

That was how our space ark failed
And how humans became extinct.

REQUIEM

REQUIEM

An eternal divide
Between sea and sky—
The gravity of existence

ACKNOWLEDGMENTS
PREVIOUSLY PUBLISHED:

"The Gravity of Loss", Winner, *WonderFold Writing Contest*, February 2018

"Sand Under a Microscope", First Place, *Angela Poetry Magazine's Poetry Contest*, May 2018

"Escape", *Noon #16*, 2020

"turning my skin", *Star*Line*, 2017

"dust carpet", *Scifaikuest*, November 2017

"keepsakes I treasure", *Scifaikuest*, May 2020

"snowy plains", *Scifaikuest*, February 2020

"unrelentlessly", *Random Planets*, 2019

"childhood monster", *Scifaikuest*, November 2015

"black moon", *Star*Line*, 2016

"a hundred", *Random Planets*, 2019

"hoping", *Star*Line*, 2017

"gritting my teeth", *Scifaikuest*, November 2018

"all my nightmares", *Scifaikuest*, November 2018

"the strange sensation", *Scifaikuest*, November 2020

"sunset", *Star*Line 39.2*, April 2016

"the second", *Scifaikuest*, February 2020

"vampiric fog", *Scifaikuest*, November 2019

"finally having fun", *Star*Line 39.2*, April 2016

"all this rain", *Star*Line 44.1, January 2021*

"mesmerized", *Scifaikuest*, November 2019

"The Joy of Traveling", *Star*Line 43.3, July 2020*

"seeing you both", *Scifaikuest*, February 2020

"the wine", *Star*Line*, 2017

"root cellar", *Grievous Angel*, 2016

"first date", *Dreams and Nightmares 106*, May 2017

"tree on a hill", *Scifaikuest*, November 2016

"sprinkled beneath", *Grievous Angel*, 6 March 2017

"Little Red in Haiku", *Star*Line 40.4*, October 2017

"red apples", *Star*Line 39.2*, April 2016

"bloody spindle", *Star*Line*, 2017
"midnight", *Star*Line*, 2017
"thrown away in recycling", *Scifaikuest*, November 2020
"even as queen", *Star*Line 42.1*, January 2019
"racing out", *Star*Line*, 2016
"after their walk", *Star*Line*, 2016
"autumn moon", *Haikuniverse*, 23 November 2016
"tornado warning", *Star*Line*, 2017
"yellow bricks", *Grievous Angel*, 17 April 2017
"pet wolf", *Star*Line*, 2017
"garage sale", *Star*Line*, 2016
"tidal waves", *Scifaikuest*, February 2020
"found in Sarpedon", *Star*Line*, 2017
"lofty silver statuettes", *Scifaikuest*, February 2016
"Marriage", *Star*Line 39.4*, October 2016
"soft whispers", *Scifaikuest*, May 2019
"standing still", *Scifaikuest*, November 2016
"sheets flapping", *Grievous Angel*, 2016
"old photo", *Star*Line 39.4*, October 2016
"midnight", *Scifaikuest*, November 2016
"bringing", *Scifaikuest*, November 2020
"longing", *Scifaikuest*, November 2020
"witching hour", *Scifaikuest*, November 2016
"solar eclipse", *Star*Line*, 2016
"whispered words", *Scifaikuest*, February 2020
"spellbook spent", *Star*Line*, 2017
"animate dead things", *Scifaikuest*, November 2015
"Electroconvulsive Therapy Session One", *Beyond The Wall of Death: Lovecraft @ 125*, August 2015
"dead butterfly", *Scifaikuest*, August 2016
"keeping you", *Scifaikuest*, August 2017
"3D Printing", Star*Line 39.1, January 2016
"alone on the ISS", *Scifaikuest*, May 2019
"A New Earth", *Scifaikuest*, May 2020
"Ebola Virus", *Dreams and Nightmares #58*, January 2001
"kill order approved", *Scifaikuest*, November 2016
"flu pandemic", *Scifaikuest*, November 2016

"First Day of Summer", *Scifaikuest*, May 2016
"The Graveyard", *Bleached Butterfly*, September 2019
"made of star stuff", *Star*Line 39.2*, April 2016
"star clusters", *Haiku Dialogue: Ad Astra*, November 2021
"clinically dead", *Scifaikuest*, August 2018
"sky full of stars", *Scifaikuest*, August 2017
"Rare Peaceful Day", *Scifaikuest*, November 2016
"Fukushima", *Scifaikuest*, November 2016
"Chernobyl", *Star*Line*, 2016
"after", *Star*Line*, 2016
"in a flash", *Scifaikuest*, November 2019
"seconds before", *Grievous Angel*, 17 April 2017
"mega tsunami", *Scifaikuest*, May 2017
"meteor shower", *Scifaikuest*, August 2019
"All Are Welcome", *Star*Line 44.4, November 2021*
"flickering flame", *Star*Line 41.1*, Winter 2018
"the graying skies", *Random Planets*, 2019
"sun death", *Scifaikuest*, November 2016
"Life on Kepler-452b", *Scifaikuest*, November 2019
"All that We Love", *Star*Line 42.4*, 2019
"too quickly", *Scifaikuest*, November 2019
"first night", *Scifaikuest*, November 2016
"within sight", *Scifaikuest*, May 2019
"ruby sky", *Scifaikuest*, February 2017
"the song I can't", *Scifaikuest*, November 2019
"just wanting", *Scifaikuest*, August 2019
"seeing red", *Scifaikuest*, November 2018
"a world", *Star*Line 39.4*, October 2016
"still can't decide", *Scifaikuest*, November 2019
"after hypnotherapy", *Star*Line 42.1*, January 2019
"running reels of my children", *Scifaikuest*, August 2020
"silent orbit of stars", *Scifaikuest*, August 2020
"time loop", *Scifaikuest*, November 2019
"wishing", *Scifaikuest*, November 2019
"alien sapling", *Scifaikuest*, August 2019
"still biting me", *Colorado Boulevard*, August 2018

"age-old battle", Winner, *All-Out Monster Revolt's Dai Kaiju Haiku Contest*, November 2017

"during the long years", *Random Planets*, 2019

"immortality", *Star*Line*, 2019

"the many ways", *Scifaikuest*, May 2019

"in my hands", *Colorado Boulevard: Dreamscapes*, December 2018

"emerging", *Colorado Boulevard*, August 2018

"multiverse theory", *Sonic Boom 9*, 6 August 2017

"slow boat to the stars", *Scifaikuest*, February 2020

"the feeling", *Star*Line*, 2018

"our ships", *Scifaikuest*, May 2020

"Found Footage", *Ladies of Horror Flash Project*, April 2019

"an eternal divide", Third Place, *Astronomers Without Borders Global Astronomy Month AstroPoetry Contest*, 2018

Awards

"The Gravity of Loss", Winner, *WonderFold Writing Contest*, February 2018, Nomination, *Dwarf Stars*, 2019

"childhood monster", Nomination, *Dwarf Stars*, 2016

"all this rain", Nomination, *Dwarf Stars*, 2022

"red apples", Nomination, *Dwarf Stars*, 2017

"root cellar", Nomination, *Dwarf Stars*, 2017

"age old battle", Winner, *All-Out Monster Revolt's Dai Kaiju Haiku Contest*, November 2017

"an eternal divide", Third Place, *Astronomers Without Borders Global Astronomy Month AstroPoetry Contest*, 2018

"bloody spindle", Nomination, *Dwarf Stars*, 2018

"ruby sky", Nomination, *Dwarf Stars*, 2018

"seconds before", Nomination, *Dwarf Stars*, 2018

"multiverse theory", Nomination, *Dwarf Stars*, 2018

"Little Red in Haiku", Honorable Mention, *Best Horror of the Year Volume Ten*, 2018

"all my nightmares", Nomination, *Dwarf Stars*, 2019

"emerging", Nomination, *Dwarf Stars*, 2019

"Sand Under a Microscope", First Place, *Angela Poetry Magazine's Poetry Contest*, May 2018

ABOUT THE AUTHOR

Christina Sng is the three-time Bram Stoker Award-winning author of *A Collection of Nightmares* (2017), *A Collection of Dreamscapes* (2020), *Tortured Willows* (2021), Elgin Award runner-up *Astropoetry* (2017), Elgin Award nominee *An Assortment of Sky Things* (2016), and haiku chapbooks *A Constellation of Songs* (2016) and *Catku* (2016).

Her poetry, fiction, essays, and art appear in such venues as *Fantastic Stories of the Imagination, Interstellar Flight Magazine, Penumbric, Southwest Review,* and *The Washington Post,* and received many accolades, including the Jane Reichhold International Prize, The Pula Film Festival International Haiku Award, multiple nominations for the Rhysling Awards, the Dwarf Stars, the Pushcart Prize, the Elgin Award, and the Ladies of Horror Fiction Award, as well as honorable mentions in the Year's Best Fantasy and Horror, and the Best Horror of the Year.

Christina was one of the recipients of the 2021 Ladies of Horror Fiction Writers Grant. Her essay Final Girl: A Life in Horror received a 2020 Bram Stoker nomination for Superior Achievement in Short Non-fiction and her first novelette Fury made its debut in the award-winning anthology *Black Cranes: Tales of Unquiet Women* (2020).

ABOUT THE COVER ARTIST

My name is Anna Surgan and I am an artist and illustrator from Mykolaiv, Ukraine. I hold a degree as an art restorer. I have been drawing since I can remember I could hold a pencil, but for the last 15 years, I have been a professional artist, and for the latest 4 years I've been an illustrator.

And that is what I do for a living. My admiration of the aesthetics from previous decades, love for the art of Renaissance and Byzantium, and love for Ukrainian folk icons possibly come from my past as an art restorer. And this love predetermined my path as an artist and later as an illustrator.

INTERSTELLAR FLIGHT PRESS

Interstellar Flight Press is an indie speculative publishing house. We feature innovative works from the best new writers in science fiction and fantasy. In the words of Ursula K. Le Guin, we need "writers who can see alternatives to how we live now, can see through our fear-stricken society and its obsessive technologies to other ways of being, and even imagine real grounds for hope."

Find us online at www.interstellarflightpress.com.

CPSIA information can be obtained
at www.ICGtesting.com
Printed in the USA
JSHW061357210822
29486JS00002B/15